WITHDRAWN

TWO RIVERS CLASSIC POEMS

Cat Jeoffry by Christopher Smart
Kubla Khan by Samuel Taylor Coleridge
Spring Song by William Shakespeare
Winter's Song by William Shakespeare
Sumer is Icumen In by an unknown medieval author
The Drunken Boat by Arthur Rimbaud

THE BALLAD OF READING GAOL

by Oscar Wilde

Afterword by Peter Stoneley
Illustrated by Peter Hay

TWO
RIVERS
PRESS

First published in 1995 by Two Rivers Press
Second edition 2004
Third edition published in 2011 by Two Rivers Press
7 Denmark Road, Reading RG1 5PA
www.tworiverspress.com

ISBN 978-1-901677-75-1

1 2 3 4 5 6 7 8 9

British Library Cataloguing in Publication Data. A catalogue
record for this book is available from the British Library.

Two Rivers Press is represented in the UK by Inpress Ltd
and distributed by Central Books.

Cover design and lettering by Sally Castle with illustration by Peter Hay
Text design by Nadja Guggi and typeset in ITC Golden Cockerel

Printed and bound in Great Britain by Herald Chase Group, Reading

'He lay as one who lies and dreams
In a pleasant meadow-land ...'

In May of 1895, the most dazzling man of letters of the nineteenth
century was sentenced to two years with hard labour for 'acts of
gross indecency with another male person.' On his release he
moved to France, where he wrote the *Ballad*: an anguished plea
for prison reform, and a passionate expression of sympathy for
his fellow prisoners, those 'souls in pain'. Oscar Wilde's *The Ballad
of Reading Gaol* was a success from its first publication, and to
this day some of its lines are among the most famous in the
English language.

In this powerfully illustrated edition, Two Rivers Press
presents Wilde's *Ballad* alongside Peter Hay's original images.
It adds a newly-commissioned Afterword by Peter Stoneley,
which draws on unpublished material in the prison archives.

The typeface used in this book is the Golden Cockerel type
designed by Eric Gill in 1929. It was commissioned by the
Golden Cockerel Press, one of the most famous private presses
of the twentieth century, in Waltham St Lawrence near Reading.
The Golden Cockerel Press was a great patron of artists and
illustrators, making its typeface an appropriate choice for
Two Rivers Press books today.

IN MEMORIAM

C.T.W.

SOMETIME TROOPER OF

THE ROYAL HORSE GUARDS

OBIIT H.M. PRISON

READING, BERKSHIRE

7 TH JULY 1896

I.

He did not wear his scarlet coat,
    For blood and wine are red,
And blood and wine were on his hands
    When they found him with the dead,
The poor dead woman whom he loved,
    And murdered in her bed.

He walked amongst the Trial Men
    In a suit of shabby gray;
A cricket cap was on his head,
    And his step seemed light and gay;
But I never saw a man who looked
    So wistfully at the day.

I never saw a man who looked
    With such a wistful eye
Upon that little tent of blue
    Which prisoners call the sky,
And at every drifting cloud that went
    With sails of silver by.

I walked, with other souls in pain,
    Within another ring,
And was wondering if the man had done
    A great or little thing,
When a voice behind me whispered low,
    "That fellow's got to swing."

Dear Christ! the very prison walls
   Suddenly seemed to reel,
And the sky above my head became
   Like a casque of scorching steel;
And, though I was a soul in pain,
   My pain I could not feel.

I only knew what hunted thought
   Quickened his step, and why
He looked upon the garish day
   With such a wistful eye;
The man had killed the thing he loved
   And so he had to die.

*

Yet each man kills the thing he loves,
  By each let this be heard,
Some do it with a bitter look,
  Some with a flattering word,
The coward does it with a kiss,
  The brave man with a sword!

Some kill their love when they are young,
  And some when they are old;
Some strangle with the hands of Lust,
  Some with the hands of Gold:
The kindest use a knife, because
  The dead so soon grow cold.

Some love too little, some too long,
    Some sell, and others buy;
Some do the deed with many tears,
    And some without a sigh:
For each man kills the thing he loves,
    Yet each man does not die.

*

He does not die a death of shame
    On a day of dark disgrace,
Nor have a noose about his neck,
    Nor a cloth upon his face,
Nor drop feet foremost through the floor
    Into an empty space.

He does not sit with silent men
    Who watch him night and day;
Who watch him when he tries to weep,
    And when he tries to pray;
Who watch him lest himself should rob
    The prison of its prey.

He does not wake at dawn to see
    Dread figures throng his room,
The shivering Chaplain robed in white,
    The Sheriff stern with gloom,
And the Governor all in shiny black,
    With the yellow face of Doom.

He does not rise in piteous haste
    To put on convict-clothes,
While some coarse-mouthed Doctor gloats,
        and notes
    Each new and nerve-twitched pose,
Fingering a watch whose little ticks
    Are like horrible hammer-blows.

He does not know that sickening thirst
    That sands one's throat, before
The hangman with his gardener's gloves
    Slips through the padded door,
And binds one with three leathern thongs,
    That the throat may thirst no more.

He does not bend his head to hear
   The Burial Office read,
Nor, while the terror of his soul
   Tells him he is not dead,
Cross his own coffin, as he moves
   Into the hideous shed.

He does not stare upon the air
   Through a little roof of glass:
He does not pray with lips of clay
   For his agony to pass;
Nor feel upon his shuddering cheek
   The kiss of Caiaphas.

II.

Six weeks our guardsman walked the yard,
   In the suit of shabby gray:
His cricket cap was on his head,
   And his step seemed light and gay,
But I never saw a man who looked
   So wistfully at the day.

I never saw a man who looked
   With such a wistful eye
Upon that little tent of blue
   Which prisoners call the sky,
And at every wandering cloud that trailed
   Its ravelled fleeces by.

He did not wring his hands, as do
    Those witless men who dare
To try to rear the changeling Hope
    In the cave of black Despair:
He only looked upon the sun,
    And drank the morning air.

He did not wring his hands nor weep,
    Nor did he peek or pine,
But he drank the air as though it held
    Some healthful anodyne;
With open mouth he drank the sun
    As though it had been wine!

And I and all the souls in pain,
  Who tramped the other ring,
Forgot if we ourselves had done
  A great or little thing,
And watched with gaze of dull amaze
  The man who had to swing.

And strange it was to see him pass
  With a step so light and gay,
And strange it was to see him look
  So wistfully at the day,
And strange it was to think that he
  Had such a debt to pay.

*

For oak and elm have pleasant leaves
    That in the spring-time shoot;
But grim to see is the gallows-tree,
    With its adder-bitten root,
And, green or dry, a man must die
    Before it bears its fruit!

The loftiest place is that seat of grace
For which all worldlings try:
    But who would stand in hempen band
Upon a scaffold high,
    And through a murderer's collar take
His last look at the sky?

It is sweet to dance to violins
    When Love and Life are fair:
To dance to flutes, to dance to lutes
    Is delicate and rare:
But it is not sweet with nimble feet
    To dance upon the air!

So with curious eyes and sick surmise
    We watched him day by day,
And wondered if each one of us
    Would end the self-same way,
For none can tell to what red Hell
    His sightless soul may stray.

*

At last the dead man walked no more
    Amongst the Trial Men,
And I knew that he was standing up
    In the black dock's dreadful pen,
And that never would I see his face
    In God's sweet world again.

Like two doomed ships that pass in storm
    We had crossed each other's way:
But we made no sign, we said no word,
    We had no word to say;
For we did not meet in the holy night,
    But in the shameful day.

A prison wall was round us both,
    Two outcast men we were:
The world had thrust us from its heart,
    And God from out His care:
And the iron gin that waits for Sin
    Had caught us in its snare.

III.

In Debtor's Yard the stones are hard,
    And the dripping wall is high,
So it was there he took the air
    Beneath the leaden sky,
And by each side a Warder walked,
    For fear the man might die.

Or else he sat with those who watched
    His anguish night and day;
Who watched him when he rose to weep,
    And when he crouched to pray;
Who watched him lest himself should rob
    Their scaffold of its prey.

The Governor was strong upon
    The Regulations Act:
The Doctor said that Death was but
    A scientific fact:
And twice a day the Chaplain called,
    And left a little tract.

And twice a day he smoked his pipe,
    And drank his quart of beer:
His soul was resolute, and held
    No hiding-place for fear;
He often said that he was glad
    The hangman's hands were near.

But why he said so strange a thing
    No Warder dared to ask:
For he to whom a watcher's doom
    Is given as his task,
Must set a lock upon his lips,
    And make his face a mask.

Or else he might be moved, and try
  To comfort or console:
And what should Human Pity do
  Pent up in Murderers' Hole?
What word of grace in such a place
  Could help a brother's soul?

*

With slouch and swing around the ring
  We trod the Fools' Parade!
We did not care: we knew we were
  The Devil's Own Brigade:
And shaven head and feet of lead
  Make a merry masquerade.

We tore the tarry rope to shreds
   With blunt and bleeding nails;
We rubbed the doors, and scrubbed the floors,
   And cleaned the shining rails:
And, rank by rank, we soaped the plank,
   And clattered with the pails.

We sewed the sacks, we broke the stones,
   We turned the dusty drill:
We banged the tins, and bawled the hymns,
   And sweated on the mill:
But in the heart of every man
   Terror was lying still.

So still it lay that every day
　　Crawled like a weed-clogged wave:
And we forgot the bitter lot
　　That waits for fool and knave,
Till once, as we tramped in from work,
　　We passed an open grave.

With yawning mouth the yellow hole
　　Gaped for a living thing;
The very mud cried out for blood
　　To the thirsty asphalte ring:
And we knew that ere one dawn grew fair
　　Some prisoner had to swing.

Right in we went, with soul intent
    On Death and Dread and Doom:
The hangman, with his little bag,
    Went shuffling through the gloom:
And each man trembled as he crept
    Into his numbered tomb.

*

That night the empty corridors
    Were full of forms of Fear,
And up and down the iron town
    Stole feet we could not hear,
And through the bars that hide the stars
    White faces seemed to peer.

He lay as one who lies and dreams
  In a pleasant meadow-land,
The watchers watched him as he slept,
  And could not understand
How one could sleep so sweet a sleep
  With a hangman close at hand.

But there is no sleep when men must weep
  Who never yet have wept:
So we – the fool, the fraud, the knave –
  That endless vigil kept,
And through each brain on hands of pain
  Another's terror crept.

*

Alas! it is a fearful thing
  To feel another's guilt!
For, right within, the sword of Sin
  Pierced to its poisoned hilt,
And as molten lead were the tears we shed
  For the blood we had not spilt.

The Warders with their shoes of felt
  · Crept by each padlocked door,
And peeped and saw, with eyes of awe,
  Gray figures on the floor,
And wondered why men knelt to pray
  Who never prayed before.

All through the night we knelt and prayed,
   Mad mourners of a corse!
The troubled plumes of midnight were
   The plumes upon a hearse:
And bitter wine upon a sponge
   Was the savour of Remorse.

*

The gray cock crew, the red cock crew,
   But never came the day:
And crooked shapes of Terror crouched,
   In the corners where we lay:
And each evil sprite that walks by night
   Before us seemed to play.

They glided past, they glided fast,
  Like travellers through a mist:
They mocked the moon in a rigadoon
  Of delicate turn and twist,
And with formal pace and loathsome grace
  The phantoms kept their tryst.

With mop and mow, we saw them go,
  Slim shadows hand in hand:
About, about, in ghostly rout
  They trod a saraband:
And the damned grotesques made arabesques,
  Like the wind upon the sand!

With the pirouettes of marionettes,
   They tripped on pointed tread:
But with flutes of Fear they filled the ear,
   As their grisly masque they led,
And loud they sang, and long they sang,
   For they sang to wake the dead.

"Oho!" they cried, *"The world is wide,*
   But fettered limbs go lame!
And once, or twice, to throw the dice
   Is a gentlemanly game,
But he does not win who plays with Sin
   In the secret House of Shame."

No things of air these antics were,
  That frolicked with such glee:
To men whose lives were held in gyves,
  And whose feet might not go free,
Ah! wounds of Christ! they were living things,
  Most terrible to see.

Around, around, they waltzed and wound;
  Some wheeled in smirking pairs;
With the mincing step of a demirep
  Some sidled up the stairs:
And with subtle sneer, and fawning leer,
  Each helped us at our prayers.

*

The morning wind began to moan,
   But still the night went on:
Through its giant loom the web of gloom
   Crept till each thread was spun:
And, as we prayed, we grew afraid
   Of the Justice of the Sun.

The moaning wind went wandering round
   The weeping prison-wall:
Till like a wheel of turning steel
   We felt the minutes crawl:
O moaning wind! what had we done
   To have such a seneschal?

At last I saw the shadowed bars,
  Like a lattice wrought in lead,
Move right across the whitewashed wall
  That faced my three-plank bed,
And I knew that somewhere in the world
  God's dreadful dawn was red.

*

At six o'clock we cleaned our cells,
  At seven all was still,
But the sough and swing of a mighty wing
  The prison seemed to fill,
For the Lord of Death with icy breath
  Had entered in to kill.

He did not pass in purple pomp,
    Nor ride a moon-white steed.
Three yards of cord and a sliding board
    Are all the gallows' need:
So with rope of shame the Herald came
    To do the secret deed.

*

We were as men who through a fen
    Of filthy darkness grope:
We did not dare to breathe a prayer,
    Or to give our anguish scope:
Something was dead in each of us,
    And what was dead was Hope.

For Man's grim Justice goes its way,
　　And will not swerve aside:
It slays the weak, it slays the strong,
　　It has a deadly stride:
With iron heel it slays the strong,
　　The monstrous parricide!

*

We waited for the stroke of eight:
　　Each tongue was thick with thirst:
For the stroke of eight is the stroke of Fate
　　That makes a man accursed,
And Fate will use a running noose
　　For the best man and the worst.

We had no other thing to do,
    Save to wait for the sign to come:
So, like things of stone in a valley lone,
    Quiet we sat and dumb:
But each man's heart beat thick and quick
    Like a madman on a drum!

                    *

With sudden shock the prison-clock
    Smote on the shivering air,
And from all the gaol rose up a wail
    Of impotent despair,
Like the sound that frightened marshes hear
    From some leper in his lair.

And as one sees most fearful things
    In the crystal of a dream,
We saw the greasy hempen rope
    Hooked to the blackened beam,
And heard the prayer the hangman's snare
    Strangled into a scream.

And all the woe that moved him so
    That he gave that bitter cry,
And the wild regrets, and the bloody sweats,
    None knew so well as I:
For he who lives more lives than one
    More deaths than one must die.

IV.

There is no chapel on the day
    On which they hang a man:
The Chaplain's heart is far too sick,
    Or his face is far to wan,
Or there is that written in his eyes
    Which none should look upon.

So they kept us close till nigh on noon,
    And then they rang the bell,
And the Warders with their jingling keys
    Opened each listening cell,
And down the iron stair we tramped,
    Each from his separate Hell.

Out into God's sweet air we went,
　　But not in wonted way,
For this man's face was white with fear,
　　And that man's face was gray,
And I never saw sad men who looked
　　So wistfully at the day.

I never saw sad men who looked
　　With such a wistful eye
Upon that little tent of blue
　　We prisoners called the sky,
And at every careless cloud that passed
　　In happy freedom by.

But there were those amongst us all
    Who walked with downcast head,
And knew that, had each got his due,
    They should have died instead:
He had but killed a thing that lived,
    Whilst they had killed the dead.

For he who sins a second time
    Wakes a dead soul to pain,
And draws it from its spotted shroud,
    And makes it bleed again,
And makes it bleed great gouts of blood,
    And makes it bleed in vain!

*

Like ape or clown, in monstrous garb
  With crooked arrows starred,
Silently we went round and round
  The slippery asphalte yard;
Silently we went round and round,
  And no man spoke a word.

Silently we went round and round,
  And through each hollow mind
The Memory of dreadful things
  Rushed like a dreadful wind,
And Horror stalked before each man,
  And Terror crept behind.

*

The Warders strutted up and down,
    And kept their herd of brutes,
Their uniforms were spick and span,
    And they wore their Sunday suits,
But we knew the work they had been at,
    By the quicklime on their boots.

For where a grave had opened wide,
    There was no grave at all:
Only a stretch of mud and sand
    By the hideous prison-wall,
And a little heap of burning lime,
    That the man should have his pall.

For he has a pall, this wretched man,
    Such as few men can claim:
Deep down below a prison-yard,
    Naked for greater shame,
He lies, with fetters on each foot,
    Wrapt in a sheet of flame!

And all the while the burning lime
    Eats flesh and bone away,
It eats the brittle bone by night,
    And the soft flesh by day,
It eats the flesh and bones by turns,
    But it eats the heart alway.

*

For three long years they will not sow
    Or root or seedling there:
For three long years the unblessed spot
    Will sterile be and bare,
And look upon the wondering sky
    With unreproachful stare.

They think a murderer's heart would taint
    Each simple seed they sow.
It is not true! God's kindly earth
    Is kindlier than men know,
And the red rose would but blow more red,
    The white rose whiter blow.

Out of his mouth a red, red rose!
  Out of his heart a white!
For who can say by what strange way,
  Christ brings His will to light,
Since the barren staff the pilgrim bore
  Bloomed in the great Pope's sight?

*

But neither milk-white rose nor red
  May bloom in prison air;
The shard, the pebble, and the flint,
  Are what they give us there:
For flowers have been known to heal
  A common man's despair.

So never will wine-red rose or white,
  Petal by petal, fall
On that stretch of mud and sand that lies
  By the hideous prison-wall,
To tell the men who tramp the yard
  That God's Son died for all.

*

Yet though the hideous prison-wall
  Still hems him round and round,
And a spirit may not walk by night
  That is with fetters bound,
And a spirit may but weep that lies
  In such unholy ground,

He is at peace – this wretched man –
    At peace, or will be soon:
There is no thing to make him mad,
    Nor does Terror walk at noon,
For the lampless Earth in which he lies
    Has neither Sun nor Moon.

They hanged him as a beast is hanged:
    They did not even toll
A requiem that might have brought
    Rest to his startled soul,
But hurriedly they took him out,
    And hid him in a hole.

They stripped him of his canvas clothes,
    And gave him to the flies:
They mocked the swollen purple throat,
    And the stark and staring eyes:
And with laughter loud they heaped the shroud
    In which their convict lies.

The Chaplain would not kneel to pray
    By his dishonoured grave:
Nor mark it with that blessed cross
    That Christ for sinners gave,
Because the man was one of those
    Whom Christ came down to save.

Yet all is well; he has but passed
   To Life's appointed bourne:
And alien tears will fill for him
   Pity's long-broken urn,
For his mourners will be outcast men,
   And outcasts always mourn.

V.

I know not whether Laws be right,
   Or whether Laws be wrong;
All that we know who lie in gaol
   Is that the wall is strong;
And that each day is like a year,
   A year whose days are long.

But this I know, that every Law
    That men hath made for Man,
Since first Man took his brother's life
    And the sad world began,
But straws the wheat and saves the chaff
    With a most evil fan.

This too I know – and wise it were
    If each could know the same –
That every prison that men build
    Is built with bricks of shame,
And bound with bars lest Christ should see
    How men their brothers maim.

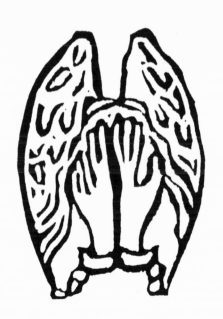

With bars they blur the gracious moon,
  And blind the goodly sun:
And they do well to hide their Hell,
  For in it things are done
That Son of God nor son of Man
  Ever should look upon!

*

The vilest deeds like poison weeds
  Bloom well in prison-air:
It is only what is good in Man
  That wastes and withers there:
Pale Anguish keeps the heavy gate,
  And the Warder is Despair.

For they starve the little frightened child
    Till it weeps both night and day:
And they scourge the weak, and flog the fool,
    And gibe the old and gray,
And some grow mad, and all grow bad,
    And none a word may say.

Each narrow cell in which we dwell
    Is a foul and dark latrine,
And the fetid breath of living Death
    Chokes up each grated screen,
And all, but Lust, is turned to dust
    In Humanity's machine.

The brackish water that we drink
    Creeps with a loathsome slime,
And the bitter bread they weigh in scales
    Is full of chalk and lime,
And Sleep will not lie down, but walks
    Wild-eyed, and cries to Time.

*

But though lean Hunger and green Thirst
    Like asp with adder fight,
We have little care of prison fare,
    For what chills and kills outright
Is that every stone one lifts by day
    Becomes one's heart by night.

With midnight always in one's heart,
    And twilight in one's cell,
We turn the crank, or tear the rope,
    Each in his separate Hell,
And the silence is more awful far
    Than the sound of a brazen bell.

And never a human voice comes near
    To speak a gentle word:
And the eye that watches through the door
    Is pitiless and hard:
And by all forgot, we rot and rot,
    With soul and body marred.

And thus we rust Life's iron chain
   Degraded and alone:
And some men curse, and some men weep,
   And some men make no moan:
But God's eternal Laws are kind
   And break the heart of stone.

*

And every human heart that breaks,
   In prison cell or yard,
Is as that broken box that gave
   Its treasure to the Lord,
And filled the unclean leper's house
   With the scent of costliest nard.

Ah! happy they whose hearts can break
    And peace of pardon win!
How else may man make straight his plan
    And cleanse his soul from Sin?
How else but through a broken heart
    May Lord Christ enter in?

                    *

And he of the swollen purple throat.
    And the stark and staring eyes,
Waits for the holy hands that took
    The Thief to Paradise;
And a broken and a contrite heart
    The Lord will not despise.

The man in red who reads the Law
    Gave him three weeks of life,
Three little weeks in which to heal
    His soul of his soul's strife,
And cleanse from every blot of blood
    The hand that held the knife.

And with tears of blood he cleansed the hand,
    The hand that held the steel:
For only blood can wipe out blood,
    And only tears can heal:
And the crimson stain that was of Cain
    Became Christ's snow-white seal.

VI.

In Reading gaol by Reading town
    There is a pit of shame,
And in it lies a wretched man
    Eaten by teeth of flame,
In burning winding-sheet he lies,
    And his grave has got no name.

And there, till Christ call forth the dead,
   In silence let him lie:
No need to waste the foolish tear,
   Or heave the windy sigh:
The man had killed the thing he loved,
   And so he had to die.

And all men kill the thing they love,
   By all let this be heard,
Some do it with a bitter look,
   Some with a flattering word,
The coward does it with a kiss,
   The brave man with a sword!

C. 3. 3

NOTES

The Ballad of Reading Gaol was first published in London on
February 13, 1898 by Leonard Smithers. Wilde's name was not
given as author, but his prison number, C.3.3, appeared on the
title-page. Wilde made a number of changes for the second
edition, published again by Smithers, on 2nd March 1898.
Changes have been made to the first Two Rivers Press edition
to bring the current text into line with the second edition
as corrected by Wilde. For a full textual history of the *Ballad*,
including textual variants and explanatory notes, see *The
Complete Works of Oscar Wilde I: Poems and Poems in Prose*, ed. Bobby
Fong and Karl Beckson (Oxford: Oxford University Press, 2000),
pp. 195–315.

Trial Men: those awaiting trial, as opposed to those that had been
   tried and sentenced.
cricket cap: prisoners were required to wear caps with low peaks,
   to prevent them from making eye-contact with and talking to
   each other.
another ring: prisoners took exercise by walking round in circles,
   though perhaps Wilde is also drawn to the phrase because it
   suggests Dante's circles or rings of Hell.
a little roof of glass: the place of execution in the 1890s was also
   where the 'mugshots' were taken. Wilde seems not to have
   realised the dual purpose. In a letter to Robert Ross, he
   comments on the fact that the execution shed had a glass
   roof 'like a photographer's studio on the sands at Margate.
   For eighteen months I thought it *was* the studio for
   photographing prisoners' (*Letters*, 956).
shoes of felt: in these shoes the warders could approach
   prisoners without being heard, and catch them in any
   breaking of the rules.
the barren staff the pilgrim bore: in legend, and specifically
   in ballads, it is the Pope's staff that blossoms, after a visit
   from Tannhäuser.

AFTERWORD
Oscar Wilde and *The Ballad of Reading Gaol*

In the 1890s, the crimes of those locked up in Her Majesty's
Prison, Reading, ranged from the petty – stealing bread, a whip,
an accordion, handkerchiefs, rabbits, a pot of jam – to murder.
The sentences ranged from seven days' imprisonment for theft,
to death by hanging for the murder. On November 20, 1895, the
most dazzling man of letters of the nineteenth century joined
this company.

Oscar Wilde was born in Dublin on October 16, 1854, the son
of an eminent surgeon and an Irish patriot poet. He was given a
classical education at a leading Irish school, and at Trinity College
Dublin. With the benefit of a scholarship, he went on to Oxford
University, where he won the Newdigate Prize for poetry and
graduated with first class honours. The scholar and poet rapidly
transformed himself into a playwright, essayist, and literary
celebrity. At the time of his arrest, Wilde had two popular plays,
An Ideal Husband and *The Importance of Being Earnest*, running in
the West End of London.

Although Wilde was married and had two sons, in 1891 he
became involved in a love affair with the twenty-one-year-old
Lord Alfred Douglas. Through the early 1890s, he also paid
for sexual encounters with young men of a much lower class.
These men were in their late teens and early twenties, and
alongside their activities as prostitutes and blackmailers,
they often maintained regular working lives as grooms and
messengers. Aside from paying in cash, Wilde also gave expensive
gifts to the young men, and especially in the form of silver
cigarette cases. Douglas's father, the Marquess of Queensberry,
began an aggressive campaign of harassment towards Wilde,
trying to disrupt the opening night of *The Importance of Being
Earnest*, and leaving a poorly-spelled card at the Albemarle Club,
'To Oscar Wilde posing as a somdomite'. Wilde sued for libel,

which was unwise. Whether he was 'posing' as a 'sodomite' or
not, he was a practising homosexual. In suing Queensberry, he
would have to commit what he would later describe as 'absurd
and silly perjuries' (*Letters*, 691). At the libel trial, Queensberry's
defence provided evidence to suggest Wilde's sexual relation-
ships with young men. Wilde also seemed to declare his own
guilt. The defence barrister, Edward Carson, asked whether
he had ever kissed a sixteen-year-old servant. Wilde, perhaps
relieved to be able to tell the truth for once, said a great deal
too much: 'Oh dear no! He was a peculiarly plain boy' (*Trials*, 133).
Carson was then able to suggest that Wilde was, by his own
indirect admission, in the habit of kissing boys who were
not plain.

Queensberry's defence counsel intended to put a number of
young men in the witness box to testify that they had had, or
knew of sexual encounters with Wilde. Given that the trial
was already turning against the playwright, his barrister urged
him to surrender his case, which he did. But too much had
already been uncovered. Queensberry's solicitor contacted the
Director of Public Prosecutions with information about what
the witnesses would have said, had the trial continued. Under
the Home Secretary's direction, Wilde was arrested and tried in
his turn. In his first trial as defendant, the jury failed to reach a
verdict. But on May 25, 1895, at the end of a second trial, he was
found guilty. Sent to Newgate Prison, he was transferred to
Pentonville and Wandsworth, and then to Reading, where he
would serve out the majority of his sentence.

There had been statutes against 'buggery' in English criminal
law since 1533, and in ecclesiastical law for centuries before that.
It had been punishable by death. But 'buggery' was a vague term,
signifying 'abominable heresy', and it covered a variety of acts,
including bestiality, and anal sex between men and women.
The last execution for buggery had been in 1836. The death
penalty was removed in 1861, to be replaced with a minimum
jail term of ten years. Wilde fell victim to a new and more

targeted instrument of victimisation. He was found guilty under Article XI of the Criminal Law Amendment Act of 1885, which was specifically directed at sex between men, but not including the most serious offence of anal penetration. The Act had been intended to protect girls and young women from prostitution, following reports in the press about girls working in brothels. Article XI was added as something of an afterthought by Henry Labouchère, and slipped through under pressure of other business. The notorious 'Labouchère Amendment' specified 'acts of gross indecency with another male person'. Decent means 'fitting' or 'proper to the circumstances', which might seem to imply public behaviour – fitting to be witnessed by others without giving offence. But sex between men was considered 'indecent' when it took place between consenting adults in a private place. There were no 'proper' circumstances of any kind.

Wilde, then, was not convicted for having sex with men who were under-age, or for having paid for sexual services. There was no age of consent for same-sex relations, though those with whom Wilde had sex would seem to have been above the present-day United Kingdom age of consent of sixteen. The simple fact that he had had a sexual encounter with another man made him liable to a maximum sentence of two years' hard labour, and he was given the maximum sentence.

*

Wilde was an aesthete who urged 'art for art's sake'. Echoing – sometimes copying from – earlier aesthetes from Gautier to Pater and Whistler, he spoke against the idea of art as a means of social and moral control. He famously declared in the Preface to the second version of *The Picture of Dorian Gray* (1891):

> There is no such thing as a moral or an immoral book. Books are well written, or they are badly written. That is all ...
> No artist desires to prove anything ... No artist has ethical sympathies. (*Picture*, 167)

He was reacting against stifling and prudish Victorian moral conventions. According to Wilde, it was not the artist's role to be 'good' or to make others 'good'. Nor was it to attempt to address social injustice. Art, rather, was a 'shield' against 'the sordid perils of actual existence' ('Critic', 173). His experiences in Reading Prison would not lead him to embrace conventional morality, but they would cause him to write with 'ethical sympathies', and to take up social causes.

To walk into the central hall of the prison – it is now a young offenders' institution and remand centre – is to enter an airy, ecclesiastical space, with three wings of arched ceilings and gothic windows. To go into a cell, however, is to enter a small, bare compartment. The door is heavy and narrow, and the depth of the window cavity reveals the thickness of the prison walls. Wilde, like most prisoners, spent the majority of his time in solitary confinement, and when out of his cell he was not allowed to talk to others. He had been condemned to hard labour, which usually meant stone-breaking, the treadmill, or picking oakum. The first two were exhausting, while picking oakum – the unravelling of tarry strands of old rope – was brutally dull, and led, as Wilde put it in his poem, to 'blunt and bleeding nails'. In the event he was more fortunate, in part because his health broke down. He was given the tasks of helping in the garden and aiding the 'schoolmaster's orderly'. But with or without hard labour it was a bitter regime. As he would write after his release, in a letter to the *Daily Chronicle*:

> Deprived of books, of all human intercourse, isolated from every human and humanising influence, condemned to eternal silence, robbed of all intercourse with the external world, treated like an unintelligent animal, brutalised below the level of any brute-creation, the wretched man who is confined in an English prison can hardly escape becoming insane. (*Letters*, 1047)

However calm and airy the old prison building might seem to the modern visitor, in his campaigning letters to the *Chronicle*

Wilde wrote of the unsanitary 'slops' arrangements which, along with the lack of ventilation, caused the warders to be 'violently sick' when they came on duty (*Letters*, 1046). He also wrote of the fact that children were kept in prison – 'quite small children' – and that the 'cruelty that is practiced by day and night on children in English prisons is incredible' (*Letters*, 848).

*

Shortly after his release on May 19, 1897, Wilde moved to Berneval near Dieppe. There, he began his most ambitious and most successful attempt at prison reform, *The Ballad of Reading Gaol*. It is dedicated to and tells the story of 'C. T. W.', or Charles Thomas Wooldridge, a trooper who was hanged in Reading Prison on July 7, 1896. Wooldridge had murdered his wife, cutting her throat in a jealous rage.

Wilde exploits the ballad tradition with tremendous skill. His stanzas are longer than in traditional ballads, but he keeps the same powerful rhythms and evocative reiterations. In adopting the story of Wooldridge, he also observes the ballad's tendency to focus on love that ends with a dramatic and violent episode. Wilde takes liberties with the facts, choosing to picture Wooldridge in a 'scarlet coat' even though, as a trooper in the Royal Horse Guards, Wooldridge was a member of the 'Blues'. He also has the trooper murder his wife in the emblematic scene of betrayal, their bed, when newspaper reports indicate that he killed her in the street near their home. The drama of the poem is psychological, in that it describes the gruesome experience of waiting for the death-sentence to be carried out. This invites the underlying moral of the poem – that punishment is seldom born equally or fairly, and that it is the trooper's fate to embody a universal guilt.

Wilde, his friends, and the critics all agreed that the poem was, artistically, no more than a partial success. The poet himself saw it as an awkward mix, 'some poetry, some propaganda' (*Letters*, 956). But the reviews were generally favourable, and the poem had gone through seven editions by 1899. It had been published under Wilde's prison number, C.3.3, until 1899, but his authorship was widely surmised. Given the infamy that now attached to his name, Wilde thought that 'the Press ha[d] behaved very well' (*Letters*, 1041).

The Ballad of Reading Gaol was soon being quoted in Parliament in debates over prison reform, and, ever since, Wilde's words have served as rallying cries for campaigners. Perhaps this is what he and his contemporaries most failed to realise about the *Ballad* – that he had struck upon images and phrases that are so bold, so laden with colour and intensity, that they are unforgettable. Whether it is the statement that 'each man kills the thing he loves', or the reference to the 'little tent of blue' which 'prisoners call the sky', the *Ballad* contains lines that are now among the most familiar in English literature. The poem has a prophetic and allegorical power which is equal to the power of wit to be found in *The Importance of Being Earnest*. It also evokes in subtle but compelling terms the theme of same-sex love. All the prisoners participate in the agonies that must be endured by the poem's hero, and all experience the shame of the final event. The 'romance' lies in the love between the man and wife that ends in murder, but also in the secret, unspoken sharing between the 'outcast men' in the prison.

Whether one would have wished him to or not – and his friends certainly wished him to – Wilde did not change. Soon after his release from prison he was chasing 'boys' again with Alfred Douglas, this time in Naples. The final phase of love and shared enthusiasms with Douglas did not last long. Wilde's subsequent years were marked by loneliness, ill health, and shabby gentility. There was to be little further writing. In his *Ballad*, though – the poem he described as his '*chant de cygne*' or swan song (*Letters*, 1035) – he brought attention to the cruel and counter-productive treatment of prisoners, many of those prisoners mentally unstable, many of them children, many convicted of petty crimes. In the midst of wonderfully effective 'propaganda', he produced his finest

'romance', and achieved the tragic eloquence for which he had
often strived, but which had, until that point, escaped him.

Peter Stoneley

*Peter Stoneley is a Professor in the Department of English Language and
Literature at the University of Reading. He specialises in American literature
and culture, and queer studies. His books include* Consumerism and
American Girls' Literature *(Cambridge University Press, 2003), and*
A Queer History of the Ballet *(Routledge, 2007).*

WORKS CITED

Merlin Holland and Rupert Hart-Davis, eds. *The Complete Letters
of Oscar Wilde.* London: Fourth Estate, 2000

H. Mongomery Hyde. *The Trials of Oscar Wilde.* New York: Dover, 1973

Oscar Wilde. 'The Critic as Artist', *The Complete Works of Oscar Wilde*,
Volume 4. Ed. Josephine M. Guy. Oxford: Oxford University Press,
2007

— *The Picture of Dorian Gray*, in *The Complete Works of Oscar Wilde*,
Volume 3. Ed. Joseph Bristow. Oxford: Oxford University Press, 2005

FURTHER READING

Although it has been contested by later work, Richard Ellmann's
Oscar Wilde (London: Hamish Hamilton, 1987) remains the standard
biography. Karl Beckson's *The Oscar Wilde Encyclopedia* (New York:
AMS, 1998) is a very useful reference guide to all aspects of Wilde's
life and works. For a detailed history of Reading Prison, including
much material on the period of Wilde's incarceration, see Anthony
Stokes, *Pit of Shame* (Winchester: Waterside, 2007). Regenia Gagnier
provides a fascinating Marxist-inspired treatment of aestheticism
in *Idylls of the Marketplace* (Stanford: Stanford University Press, 1986).
For a brief essay on the ballad form, see *The Princeton Encyclopedia
of Poetry and Poetics*, ed. Alex Preminger (Princeton, New Jersey:
Princeton University Press, 1974).

Two Rivers Press has been publishing in and about Reading since 1994. Founded by the artist Peter Hay (1951–2003), the press continues to delight readers, local and further afield, with its varied list of individually designed, thought-provoking books.

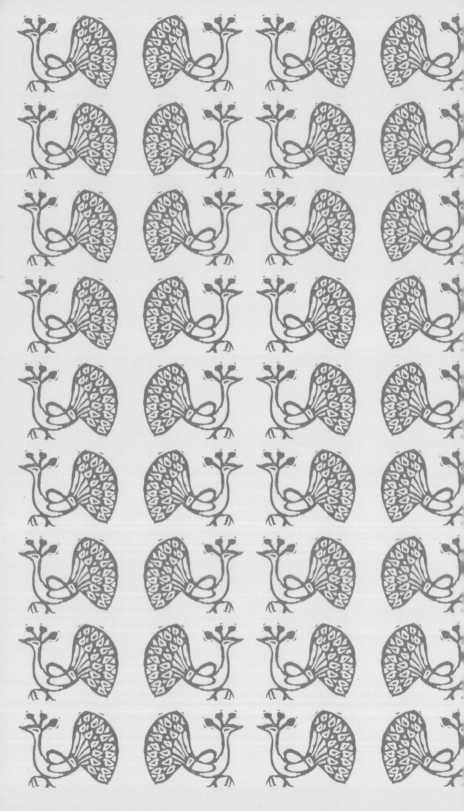